The Windermere Way

Judy Law

Foreword by John Jacobi

Documentary Media
Seattle, Washington

The Windermere Way

Published by Documentary Media
3250 41st Ave SW
Seattle WA 98116
206 935-9292
books@docbooks.com
www.documentarymedia.com

First edition 2007
Printed in Canada

Author: Judy Law
Foreword: John Jacobi
Editors: Judy Gouldthorpe, Barbara Edmondson
Design: Paul Langland Design

Library of Congress Cataloging-in-Publication Data
Law, Judy
The Windermere way / Judy Law ; foreword by John Jacobi.
    p. cm.
ISBN 978-1-933245-06-5
1. Real estate business—Management. I. Title.

HD1375.L39 2007
333.330979—dc22

2006101232

Table of Contents

*I dedicate this book
to my mother and father,
Joie and Lee Jacobi.*

John Jacobi

In a favorite family photo, Zee and Joie Jacobi are dressed in tropical attire for a costume party in the late 1960s.

Foreword

My first business lesson has stayed with me throughout the years. As a loan officer in my early days with a bank, I presented applications to the loan committee members. At one point, I was trying to explain why I thought we should turn down an applicant, and I vividly recall the chairman of the bank cutting me off and saying, "Young man, give me reasons for approving the loan, not why we shouldn't. We're in the business of making loans!" Since that day, I've looked for ways to make things happen — even when it wasn't the way things were done.

Another key lesson that has served me well was realizing I didn't have to know it all or be the smartest. As long as I worked with others who had talents and skills that I didn't have, then together we could make the right decisions and achieve things I couldn't if I were on my own.

I've learned, too, that in building a strong, sound business, trying new things is as important as hanging on to the things that you know work. This has allowed me to not fear making mistakes. We gain considerably from our mistakes, and if something doesn't work, we can change it quickly. In order to be successful, you have to throw out the rules, rebuild, renovate.

These are some of the lessons I learned early on, and they've become part of the fabric of Windermere. There's so much knowledge and wisdom gained from great people and their experiences that I wanted to tell the story of Windermere's history, how its business philosophies were born, and how a "Windermere Way" culture has developed over the years. Certainly, I wanted to do it so that as our company grows, the owners and agents recognize that the things we did and believed in at the beginning are just as important and fundamental today.

I hope those who read these stories will enjoy them and understand. It used to be that I could personally talk to all the owners and managers and salespeople, discuss things, toss around ideas.

For obvious reasons, I can't do that anymore. But I want the people of Windermere to know, understand, and — if willing — embrace the Windermere philosophies and culture expressed in this book.

I also wanted a permanent record of the people who have been with me since the early years. Without them, their hard work and dedication, their willingness to believe in my ideas, Windermere would not have been possible. This book acknowledges those who helped build this company. To them I give my heartfelt appreciation. They were — and still are — the essential reason why there is a story to tell.

John Jacobi

Seattle, October 2006

Thank you to my longtime personal friends who were there with me prior to Windermere. You have been instrumental in contributing to Windermere's culture and success.

George Berkman

John Coart

Jane Deasy

Gail Hofeditz

Rick and Patti Menti

Jim Shapiro

Tom Walthausen

IN MEMORIAM

Bobette Cosby

Don Deasy

Terry Haberbush

Vince Haugerud

Nyal Headley

Preface

I bought my first house in the early 1980s, coming late to the realization that my days of packing up a Volkswagen with all my worldly possessions were over. To me, buying my own place just seemed like paying rent for a really long time in exchange for the right to paint the walls any color I wanted. Knowing I lacked real estate savvy, my boss recommended his agent, a woman from a big national company. It went like this at the first house she showed me:

Me: The floor slants.

Agent: It's an old house.

Me: But we're standing at a 45-degree angle. Does that seem right to you?

Agent: It's an old house.

Our relationship lasted one day before she handed me off to "someone with experience representing properties more in your price range." My new agent had just received her license. You might say we learned together. And you might say I learned the hard way. Before I embarked on another house-hunting expedition, I did my research. And many years and quite a few homes later, I can report that since then, I have always worked happily with Windermere agents — they were smart and industrious, and told really good jokes.

Consequently, when I started doing advertising projects for Windermere in the late 1990s, I already held your company in high regard. Because advertising is so often about spinning and twisting and smoke

and mirrors, I also brought plenty of cynicism
with me. I had one brief meeting with
John Jacobi before starting work:

Me: I thought we'd shoot on location and
       then, if we add some special effects
       we can . . .

John: I want to use real people. Let them
       speak for themselves. Black-and-white
       film.

Me: But, don't you think . . .

John: Real people. Put 'em on a couch.
       Good meeting with you.

The honest, straightforward ad campaigns
I've been a part of since then gave me the
opportunity to interview many, many people
who've had relationships with Windermere.
Your clients love you and what your company
stands for. They respect you and trust you.
The stories I've heard from those who've
received your generosity have touched my
heart and left my cynicism in the dust. In a
business climate where suspicion abounds,
Windermere belies conventional wisdom.

Working on *The Windermere Way* has been a writer's dream. You've been candid, open, and colorful, giving me great anecdotes and memories. To all of you whom I had the opportunity to interview, my gratitude for making it easy and a whole lot of fun. My profound apologies to those I didn't interview, and especially those whose comments weren't used lest the manuscript become the length of *War and Peace*: Matt Deasy, John "O.B." Jacobi, Michael Lai, Rich Menti, Scott Wetzel, Geoff Wood, and Jill Jacobi Wood. I only wish there could be a Volume II.

To Carolyn Rathe, there couldn't be a better representative of the Windermere Way: kind, courteous, helpful, unflappable, always.

A special acknowledgment and my admiration for Maria Bunting — her meticulous research, interviews, and depth of Windermere knowledge and lore informed every chapter.

And finally, my personal and professional thanks to Lynn Pedersen, who ran this project like a champ.

Judy Law
Vashon Island, Washington

An early photo shows the flagship Windermere office at its current Sand Point Way location.

1.

Beginning

Associate with great people.

Give them a great place to work.

Give them the best tools. Pay them well.

Then, get out of their way.

John Jacobi

POLAROIDS ON THE WALLS

Orange-and-black indoor-outdoor carpet covered the floor of an area not quite 800 square feet. Metal desks sat cheek by jowl. Because practically everyone smoked everywhere in the 1970s, the place had a musty odor and the walls were an indeterminate mustard-beige. The paint color didn't matter much anyway because the walls were decorated with endless Polaroids of homes and properties for sale — including the "House of the Week," which had been prominently displayed for a year. This was Windermere Real Estate, named after the Seattle neighborhood that it served. This was the company that John Jacobi bought in 1972.

A newspaper article about Nyal Headley, the original owner of Windermere

The ambience of the place was not unique in real estate. At that time, many people in the business were dabblers and part-timers. Public perception put them in the same professional caste as white-shoed, polyester-suited used-car salesmen. Why, then, did Jacobi want to take the risk?

"I was 32 years old and had been a banker for 10 years. A part of that job I thoroughly enjoyed was creating new branches — going

16

out and finding some dirt, hiring an architect, putting up a neat new building. We were really quite good at it. But it was the bank's money, their success. In a very nice way, they were telling me what to do and how to do it. For the most part, I'm an anti-rule person. I wanted to try to do something on my own."

The Sand Point Way location before Windermere

Even though Jacobi had a wife and four children, a big mortgage, and very little money, he understood that it was a chance he just had to take. He looked at investing in a golf course, a plumbing-supply company, and a hardware store. It wasn't his aim to create some immense conglomerate. He wanted only to be on his own and generate enough income to support his family.

Jacobi heard that Windermere Real Estate was for sale. At that time, the company had a good reputation and was known for representing high-end properties. Armed with his banker's knowledge of mortgages and appraisal work, he used his own money plus a loan from his father to buy the small business.

"I've heard people gasp and laugh out loud when I've told them how much I paid for this seven-person office with nothing but a good

reputation to sell, but $85,000 was a terrific amount of money in those days," Jacobi explains. "I became the excited but anxious owner of a business I knew nothing about." His initial investment was $15,000, with the balance due in seven years.

The start-up was, to put it mildly, risky. "In the first six months we had only about 10 to 12 sales, and I'm looking at the business coming in. I can add and subtract, and I know I'm not going to be able to make my payment. I went back to appraising on the side, nights and weekends. I was scared to death."

The original Windermere business card (top) and an early yard sign. The signs were redesigned shortly after Jacobi purchased the company.

Jacobi's top salesperson was Bobette Cosby, an impeccably honest woman who did business with a handshake. She took pride in her appearance, dressing with elegant flair. (She insisted on wearing high heels well into her 80s.) It appeared at the time that she hadn't brought in any business. When John

18

finally approached Bobette with his concerns, she said, "Oh, my dear boy, I have all kinds of deals. I just haven't quite finished up." Bobette's work certainly started paying off, including a huge sale — Windermere's first-ever listing over $100,000 — to a member of the Nordstrom family. Jacobi was able to pay off his loan in just two years.

Bobette Cosby's singular approach to real estate brought Jacobi's fledgling company to a different level. "It was amazing the way she would do business," he recalls. "She'd write up transactions on napkins or matchbooks or whatever was at hand. She didn't pay a lot of attention to legalese, but that didn't matter. For Bobette, a deal with her was a deal to be trusted, no matter what. She had an amazingly loyal following; several generations of families would buy their homes from her."

Jacobi believes that Bobette's integrity and generosity showed him the way to guide Windermere. She was famous for taking care of her fellow agents. It was not unusual for her to write up and close a transaction for a colleague and then refuse to take a referral fee.

She would often lend money to young couples to help them get started. In the early days, few of the protections that exist today were in place. If there were misunderstandings at the completion — a refrigerator or an oven not included — Bobette would quietly purchase the item herself and never say a word about it.

"She was very genuine," Jacobi says. "There was no pretense, nothing phony. Her spirit and honesty were uplifting for all of us. That was just her way, and we all followed it. Bobette Cosby was exemplary in every possible sense."

Ralph Jenkins with his wife, Tiero, in Café Ralph. This social area in the Sand Point office was named for the popular mentor.

As much a part of Windermere's beginning as Bobette Cosby were two distinguished

men who had retired from the military: Ralph Jenkins and Vince Haugerud. Together, they initiated John Jacobi into the business of real estate. And they had great fun doing it.

Vince Haugerud (second from left) socializes at a Windermere golf tournament in the early 1980s.

Jacobi describes the value of these early days this way: "Windermere is often referred to as an innovative company, and that's just how we started out. When you're excited about what you're doing and want to make it better than anything else out there, you ask lots of questions and you're filled with ideas. It helped that as an outsider, I had no preconceived notions of how real estate had to be done. I kept asking questions and trying to figure out better ways of doing things or ways of differentiating ourselves. The ideas kept coming. Some worked and others were dismal failures. No matter. As long as we could keep trying to improve the way Windermere did business and we all remained flexible, then failures became lessons and in the long run, mistakes were as helpful as the successes."

THE WAY WE WERE

When John Jacobi purchased Windermere in 1972, three agents in particular were there to show him the ropes: Bobette Cosby, Vince Haugerud, and Ralph Jenkins. Betsy Lee joined in 1977. These pioneers, with their outstanding personalities and sterling professionalism, set the standard for the Windermere Way. Here are their firsthand recollections of working with John Jacobi in the early years.

Bobette Cosby: "We just had a ball."
I grew up in Seattle and graduated from the University of Washington. I worked for Windermere Real Estate for 34 years. It was John Jacobi who made it grow. He was never without an idea for something to make us larger, better, more encompassing. This was a constant. We were always selling so well, all of us, all of the time.

There was a special
rapport. We worked really
hard and we also had
wonderful parties. One par-
ticular occasion I remember
was when Ralph, Vince,

John, and I and some of the girls all came for a
luncheon and we just had a ball. We did a lot of
fun things together, like take trips to Bainbridge
Island. It was just a very compatible group of
people. We were a family. Windermere has grown so
much and it's wonderful. It's just breathtaking
what John has done.

From the day I started until the day I retired,
I loved working at Windermere. It was my life.

Vince Haugerud: "It was very simple in
those days."
I was an Air Force officer, and I first came to
Seattle with my family in 1960. We purchased a
house from Windermere and our agent was Bobette
Cosby. I went off to Africa in 1962, then came
back to Seattle in '65, and we bought again from
Bobette. Then, she called one day and asked if
I was interested in working for Windermere. I was.

23

The industry has certainly changed since then. The education and sophistication of the agents has just changed a great, great deal over all these years. It was very simple in those days. For instance, a purchase and sales agreement was just one page. We didn't have a copy machine; we used carbon paper and if we actually had to have a copy made, there was a machine down at the drugstore. Consulting with attorneys was unheard of and lawsuits were unheard of.

When John came in, he was very cooperative. He wanted to learn everything about the business. He was familiar with it from doing appraisals, but he was eager to learn all the nuts and bolts. John was always one to seek out answers, and if we ran into something we couldn't quite get our hands around, probably the next day John would come in and say what he's famous for: "I have an idea . . ." And away we'd go from there.

I feel very privileged to have been a part of this, working with John and a great group of people from the beginning. John's a man of his word and very forthright. If he says so, that's it.

Ralph Jenkins: "Once John took over, we started on an upward trajectory."

I joined Windermere Real Estate in 1969, after 32 years with the U.S. Air Force. When I started, there were four women and three men, and the owner/broker was a gentleman by the name of Nyal Headley. That was the sum total of the business. Our office was perhaps 15 feet wide and 50 feet long, with no back door. It was pretty much what you'd call a mom-and-pop operation.

About two years after I started, a young man came into the office and sat down with Nyal and they talked for a while. A few days later, Nyal told us he'd sold the company to that young man — John Jacobi. Once John took over, we started on an upward trajectory. He opened another branch office in Wedgwood, then Lake Forest Park, then Capitol Hill. It just kept going and never stopped.

There was a good feeling among the offices.
I wouldn't say it was exactly a party atmosphere,
but if an office had a party, they'd invite us and if
we did, we'd invite them. One of the best was John's
40th birthday. Rick Menti, a college buddy of
John's who later became an owner, arranged a great
surprise. Late one afternoon, cars and buses started
showing up, and out came the Husky marching
band. They assembled right in front of our office
and serenaded John. A couple of our agents got
together some cheerleader outfits and were out there
with their pom-poms. It was a great show.

John was extremely fair as a boss. Everybody
had the opportunity to do their job without nitpick-
ing interference. That was greatly appreciated by the
agents. We're all individuals and all have our own
methods within the framework of the company.
I think that permeates through Windermere — all
the way through — and it's been carried over to
today. People like to work for Windermere.

John and I are about a generation apart, but
we've always enjoyed a very, very close relationship.
Even though I retired from the business, we still go
out to lunch once a week.

Betsy Lee: "It was really the development
of family."

I started at Windermere Real Estate in 1977.

*In those days, we were just a little cubbyhole. John
had a half-dozen agents, and a couple of them were
sharing a desk.*

*John was always thinking ahead. He knew
how he wanted to run the business. He knew just
how he wanted to do things, and it was going to be
different. People said he couldn't do it. But he did.*

*The relationship among offices was very, very
close, with very little deviation from the theme.
Lots of socializing in those early days. There were
dinner parties, cruises, and get-togethers. It was
really the development of family, and he was very
determined to do that.*

*John's favorite holiday was Halloween. He had
a costume closet the likes of which you've never seen.
He could come up with the darnedest outfits — not
just masks but the clothes, the shoes, wigs, hats,
everything. He was a force to be reckoned with.*

*Windermere is still the best shop in town.
I think every agent in the Seattle area has, at one
time or another, hoped to be with Windermere.*

Pizza Pete

The expansion of Windermere proceeded in an intuitive versus acquisitive manner. It was collaborative rather than adversarial, and thoughtful instead of hurried.

Before adding to his small company, Jacobi paid a visit to Pizza Pete, a tenant in a property he managed. He had discovered that Pete Utter was an expert in franchise businesses, the man who had started one of the first and most successful operations in the early 1970s. Jacobi was intrigued by the idea that Pete earned royalties by licensing a name and a brand.

Jacobi recalls how Utter's franchise idea came to be: "Pete owned several restaurants and hired managers for each. When he visited his stores, he'd find glaring inconsistencies in the product and service, in the way the restaurants were managed, and in the physical appearance and signage both inside and out. Rather than sending down edicts from above, firing and hiring, and then having to go through the same process over and over again, he instead changed his mind-set. To ensure consistent high quality, Pete made the dough for all his restaurants in one place.

"The most revolutionary change, though, was to offer others a percentage of ownership in his restaurants. From that point on, his food was uniformly first-rate and his locations maintained a marketing-savvy, consistent appearance that built both name and product recognition with customers. It worked so well, Pete told me, because the guy or gal who takes on the responsibilities also owns the majority of financial interest. That's the same person who goes home at night and either gets to keep a hundred bucks from the day or has to worry about losing a hundred bucks." Jacobi patterned his expansion on the Pete Utter model, which rewarded entrepreneurs while ensuring the quality and reliability of the brand.

The first Windermere offices were not franchises but partnerships in the truest sense of the word. The partners maintained the majority interest while Jacobi kept a small percentage. In an exceptional agreement, he kept the voting control, even though he was the minority owner. Given this arrangement, what was to keep Jacobi from imposing his wishes on his partners, from making decisions for them? The answer, which makes MBAs cringe and lawyers flinch, is that these agreements were based solely on trust.

John Coart, Jacobi's personal attorney and close friend since high school, helped devise the agreements. He illustrates just why this maverick approach worked: "I understood the hazards going in. John was new to the industry when he acquired Windermere. That's always a risky thing, as anybody who's bought a real estate brokerage business knows, because you may buy an office that has, say, a dozen or so agents, but if you walk in the door and they don't like the way you part your hair, they might leave you with a lease and 12 empty desks. John learned the business and did a great job in developing the trust of his agents. Then, when he decided to explore expansion, he chose people he'd known and trusted before or those he'd come to know and trust through Windermere and the real estate business. He had no idea at the time just how far this was all going to go.

"John and I explored various types of business structures — corporations and partnerships and limited partnerships. We looked at allowing the owner free rein to pursue his or her entrepreneurial instincts while giving John the ability, without being too intrusive, to ensure that the company maintained the quality, image, and appearance that he believed in. That's how and why we came up with the concept of voting and non-voting stock. John selected his partners so carefully that by virtue of the trust developed, he never had to use his vote.

"John's an imaginative guy, and there were lots of times when he would have something on his mind and say, 'Geez, I would really like to do this. How can we go about it?' So I'd come up with some ideas and we'd kick them around and eventually arrive at a good way to do most of the things. It was really fun for me as a lawyer to work with someone like that."

One of the first owners and partners, Don Deasy, explains how this remarkable arrangement worked from his point of view: "We were co-owned companies and we worked in a very collegial way. The common denominator that brought us all together was John Jacobi. Sometimes we didn't agree, but when all was said and done, whatever the disagreements were going in, when we left we were all on the same page and all going the

same way. John's leadership was conveyed in a quiet way. It was all about trust. And to this day, John's never used his voting stock. The whole initial growth of Windermere was about trust and mutual respect."

Windermere grew to include 11 partners before the first real franchise operation was established — Ed Kushner on Bainbridge Island in 1984. Even then, the agreements were done differently. While other real estate companies at that time demanded 5 to 10 years from a franchise, the Windermere contract was for 30 days, at the end of which either party could terminate. (Today, the agreement period is six months due to Washington State regulations.)

This is uniquely the Windermere Way because it insists that *all* parties to the agreement be happy and successful. If the arrangement is not working, Windermere does not believe in perpetuating anyone's misery. That would be counterproductive, and simply bad business.

Jim Shapiro, the first Windermere Services Company employee, puts it more colorfully: "We didn't want anyone locked in and feeling like 'We've got you and if you leave we're going to tear off both your arms and legs and take all your money.' That's just wrong."

WE'RE GOING TO BE PARTNERS.
I said to myself, I don't want to own 50 or 60 real estate offices and have people I hired running them. I want to have somebody who owns a piece of the rock, who has the same entrepreneurial desires that I have, who goes home at night and is still worried as much as I am if they are going to make a nickel or not. We're going to be partners. I use that word over and over because it is so important. We didn't necessarily think alike. One of my first partners, Don Deasy, and I probably had more disagreements

over marketing issues and things like that, but in the end, we said, "Okay, we are going forward together." We believe in the same culture. We are not going to be splintered off. It was so terribly important to our success. I see other companies that are our competitors. They never seem to advertise together, they never do things collegially. They don't seem to make decisions together.

John Jacobi

EARLY ON

Most of the earliest Windermere owners came from professions outside real estate. Dick Baldwin was a professor at the University of Washington. Don Deasy was director of

Patti and Rick Menti

marketing for a bank. April Kieburtz was a teacher. Hugh Hoff was in management at Nordstrom. Vern Holden left the giant Transamerica Corporation to become part of the young real estate company. Rick Menti, John's fraternity brother and longtime friend, left the wholesale jewelry business to take on ownership of three offices in South Seattle. Jim Shapiro, another Windermere original, wasn't an owner but held the crucial position of first Windermere Services employee. He came from the insurance industry and learned to master myriad disciplines for the young company.

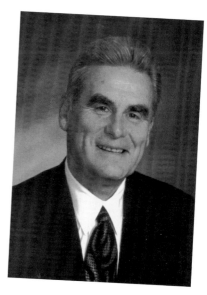

Jim Shapiro, first Services employee

These individuals, with their strong personalities and varied backgrounds, brought fresh points of view and vitality to the new company. Together, they created the foundation for Windermere's way of doing business.

All made their decision to join Windermere after careful research. Dick Baldwin, who became Jacobi's first partner, describes his experience trying to buy a home in the 1960s and how this led to his career at Windermere:

"I did my doctorate in American literature at Berkeley and came to Seattle to work at the University of Washington in 1967. We drove

around the university and stopped in a few real estate offices. That was not a very pleasant experience. Some of them, we couldn't get out of there fast enough. These were people trying to sell us every vacant dog of a property they had on the market. They were not professional and they weren't interested in us. We finally ended up at Windermere Real Estate, and Bobette Cosby was on the floor. She just did it all the right way. She cared about us. I thought then that if someone with intelligence and character wanted to start a real estate company, they could really beat the competition.

"So, when I left academia, I went to talk to Windermere. Bobette was still there, and she tried to talk me out of it, thought I should go back to teaching. She also told me I should shave off my beard. I went to work for Windermere in 1974. At the time, I was smart enough to be reasonably terrified of what I was doing. The desk I had was right outside the door to John Jacobi's office, so my training was sitting there and eavesdropping while he spoke with agents and talked on the phone. I listened to how he did it, watched how he did it. That's how I learned real estate.

"Working at Windermere in the early years was really a lot like it is now. The fundamentals were there — the collegiality, the mutual respect and sharing of information, strong management support. If all that hadn't been there then, it never could have developed later."

April Kieburtz's story is another illustrative case in point. She moved to the Northwest from Michigan in the 1970s, looking for a new career. Initially, she used her teaching background and took a job with a real estate training school. This gave her an uncommon opportunity not only to observe the business firsthand, but also to actually visit more than 300 offices in the Seattle area and to meet brokers and agents. Although she hadn't planned to go into the industry as a career, after a few months she knew she much preferred selling real estate to teaching it. Armed with an unusual depth of knowledge about real estate in Seattle, she narrowed her choices down to the three best — two of the biggest plus a small, brand-new company called Windermere. After she had interviewed at each place, Windermere was the clear choice, and she joined in the spring of 1977.

Kieburtz explains why she preferred the little start-up to the big, established entities: "The feeling at Windermere was very different from all other offices. The people were just a cut above everyone else at the other companies. At Windermere, people emanated a feeling that real estate was their true career, not an experiment. They were not there because they were bored, or because their kids had gone off to college. At Windermere, there was a tangible sense of team spirit. The people were interesting to talk to. They were extremely professional. The level of education seemed to be higher. The quality was higher."

IN THEIR OWN WORDS

The late 1970s and early '80s was a time of dramatic growth and expansion for Windermere. April Kieburtz joined in 1977 and became an early partner. Terry Haberbush started as an agent in 1982 and eventually owned five offices in the Seattle area. Ed Kushner owned an independent real estate company on Bainbridge Island, and in 1984 he was the first to join the Windermere network as a franchise owner. Here are their personal accounts of this dynamic period.

April Kieburtz: "I would have done it on a handshake because I had such complete trust in John and the rest of the guys."

Since I was there at the beginning and have been around so long, people call me the founding mother. I keep trying to get them to change it to "founding babe," but it keeps coming back around to "mother" somehow. I was never discriminated against in any way. People ask me that because initially it was three men and me around the table. But the way they were, gender never crossed my mind —

April Kieburtz

and obviously it wasn't on their radar — because I was never made to feel less.

In the very beginning you needed to be entrepreneurial; you had to be motivated. But trust and integrity to me were the biggest issues. I can remember talking about a lot of things when I was getting started, even structuring my company as it was opening. Literally, something as important as that, as critical — I would have done it on a handshake because I had such complete trust in John and the rest of the guys. And to this day, they've never failed me.

It's stimulating and exciting to be a part of the company because it is constantly evolving. We are never static. We are always creative.

Terry Haberbush: "Because we were doing things right, the best agents were attracted to us."
I came to Windermere Real Estate in 1982 as an agent at the Sand Point office. John Jacobi and Dick Baldwin were real idea guys. We'd sit around

and try to figure out how our business was going to be run in the future. We'd even storyboard how it might look. That way, Windermere was always acting rather than reacting. We were forward-looking, and we were constantly doing things and creating things that were different. We were a big departure from the norm, but we just didn't worry about what the competition was doing. If we had a good idea, we'd do it, and in a very upscale, highly ethical way. We knew we had to attract the best people to succeed, and because we were doing things right, the best agents were attracted to us.

It was exciting then because we started to grow really fast. Windermere was light-years ahead of everybody else. John is a brilliant businessman and a true visionary. There's a lot of family, not just John's but the sons and daughters of owners — the next generation — who've learned the business from the bottom up. The company is in good hands. In fact, they'll probably do it even better.

Terry Haberbush

Ed Kushner: "We were welcomed with open arms by a boatload of Windermere folks."

We had done a fair amount of business with people coming to Bainbridge Island from Seattle, and we were looking for a way to grow in that marketplace. Windermere was a better fit for us than any of the big organizations we interviewed because they were a very fluid and dynamic company. We became the first franchise in 1984.

The welcome we received consisted of several hundred Windermere people coming to Bainbridge on a boat. We walked down the street from our office and went for a cruise. We were welcomed with open arms by a boatload of Windermere folks. That was really heartening and encouraging.

A lot of the marketing materials they were producing at the time didn't fit very well in our semi-rural environment because there was an urban look and feel to them. We went through an acclimatization process together and found ways to adapt materials so they worked for us. Over time, as other franchises joined, the materials evolved even more.

When we went to Windermere owners' meetings, there was no difference between those of us who were new to the table and those who had been there a long time. There was no "us and them," no "old guard versus new guard." We were welcomed and whatever we had to say was heard, and if it was worth anything, careful attention was paid. If it wasn't worthwhile, well, then we moved on.

I had no doubt about joining Windermere then and I have absolutely no questions about it now. It was the best decision we ever made.

Ed Kushner became the first franchise owner, on Bainbridge Island, in 1984.

During a period of significant expansion and change, Windermere grew from 36 offices in 1988 to over 200 by the mid-1990s.

2.

Evolving

THE RIGHT PEOPLE

Steven Kieburtz joined Windermere as an
agent in 1980 and later became a partner,
along with his wife, April. Early in his relationship with John Jacobi, Kieburtz clearly
recalls, Jacobi made this stunning statement:
"I would be a miserable failure by myself."

Kieburtz's reaction? "I thought, 'What a
crazy thing to say. He can't really believe that.
This guy would be tremendously successful
at anything he did. He understands people.
He understands management and money and
business. He's one of the brightest guys I've
ever met.' But a ways down the road, I realized that not only did he believe it, he used it
to make this company a huge success.

"At the beginning, John understood *his*
neighborhood," Kieburtz adds. "He grew up
in the Sand Point, Lake Washington area. But
when the opportunity came up for the first

expansion on Capitol Hill, his gut reaction was that this was someone else's neighborhood, and he simply didn't have the history or roots in the community to make it work the way he wanted it to work. He needed someone who knew the Capitol Hill area and the people who lived there the way he knew Sand Point.

Steven Kieburtz

That's where Dick Baldwin came in. It was Dick's neighborhood, and he was a colleague and successful salesman. That was the idea behind local ownership, and a hallmark of Windermere's success. Windermere was and is a business about neighborhoods and communities and the people who live there."

The three disciplines of sales, service, and marketing are not separate entities at Windermere. They are so intertwined and interdependent that they might as well be one.

Just as the men and women who started
the company were mavericks, so too was
their approach to business in general and real
estate in particular.

Endemic in real estate, then and now, were
contests of all sorts. Intuitively, John Jacobi
couldn't buy into Agent of the Week or the
Month or the Year. He didn't want to award a
special parking place or prominently display
lists of what each agent had recently sold.
He talked to his agents to find out what they
thought of these competitions, and their
responses confirmed his intuition. Agents were
uncomfortable with contests because they
pitted them against each other and were a
source of jealousy and mistrust. Certainly they
were deterrents to mutual respect and
cooperation, which were the values at the core
of Jacobi's vision. He got rid of contests
and competitions. He also stopped the practice
of emblazoning business cards with self-
aggrandizing (and usually meaningless)
phrases such as "Million Dollar Producer"
and "Number 1 Agent!"

Dick Wood at Community Service Day, 1988

This evenhandedness and respect for agents, along with the company's high standards, attracted more smart and gifted people to Windermere. One of these was Dick Wood. He'd started in real estate in 1975, moving up to general manager of a large company in north Seattle. His employer was typical of the "old" way of doing business. The company was interested only in production and the bottom line. The philosophy was "Here, we got you a license, now just go out and sell something." As a result of this lack of concern, the offices were musty and unattractive; tools and support were woefully inadequate. Their agents were regarded merely as selling machines.

By 1986, Dick Wood had had enough. As a competitor, he had watched Windermere grow and had observed some important differences in the way they did business. "I noticed that their facilities were much, much nicer.

The level of professionalism in their agents was very high. They looked better, dressed better. They were a lot easier to deal with because they were friendlier and much more knowledgeable. These agents seemed to be genuinely happy. It was something you could really feel and sense from the outside."

Dick Wood met with John Jacobi, seeking a position and proposing that Windermere expand in Snohomish County. Jacobi agreed that expansion was a good idea but gave Wood no guarantees. As a next step, Steve Kieburtz mentored Wood as an agent in the Mill Creek office for over a year. This was a common practice, so the individual could learn the ways of Windermere and the company could judge whether the relationship had a good future. Jacobi describes it as being "like living together before a marriage."

Although Wood hadn't listed and sold houses for many years, he did well. He also discovered what he calls the power of Windermere. "The first week I worked for Windermere, a major Snohomish County builder called and asked me to meet with him.

He told me he thought Windermere was a classy operation with the best agents. Then he said, 'So, I'd like to give you my business.' Amazing. I knew right away that there was something really special going on. This guy was already sold on Windermere because of the people and because of what he'd seen and heard from the outside — from *his* end of the business."

Wood, who did fulfill his dream of owning a large office in Snohomish County, is convinced that the reason for the company's stellar reputation, then and now, is Windermere's belief that its agents are its most valuable assets. "What sets us apart and what is central to our success," he says, "is respect for the agents and respect for the business itself. I don't believe the other companies out there respect their agents or have much respect for this business. They just see it as a vehicle to make money."

Any question regarding Windermere's success provokes the same response: Hire the best agents. Vern Holden, who started with

Windermere in 1989 and owns the Mill Creek office, provides another eloquent description: "I hire personality. I can teach knowledge, but I can't teach someone to be a good person, an honest person. I can't make them have chemistry that fits us and works well with our team.

Vern Holden

I look for people who are optimistic, who are eager and energetic. I make sure they understand that they have to be prepared to make sacrifices, both financially and emotionally, to make it in real estate. I tell them they have a responsibility when they come to work for Windermere to perpetuate what has already been created. This is not a one-way street.

"To me the single most important word in the human vocabulary should be *we*, not *I*," Holden adds. "I think there are many ills in the world that exist as a result of too many of the 'I come first' personalities. So, if you want to be a team player, if you can contribute to the professionalism and the image that Windermere has worked so hard to create and maintain, then we can teach you what you need to know to sell real estate and be successful at it.

"I've fired more big producers than I have those who bring in far less, simply because I couldn't stand what some of those top producers turned into. Some became conspiratorial, disagreeable, and backstabbing."

Windermere agents are a reflection and an extension of the original spirit of the company. Independent thinking, creative problem-solving, and the sharing of knowledge and information are fundamental tenets. The company's success is driven by the simple fact that its people are — first and foremost — good, honest human beings. This all drives success. And what naturally follows is superb client service.

BAD AGENT

*When I bought Windermere Real Estate, the first
thing I was trying to learn and do better was
getting the right people. I'd go home after hiring
somebody great and think, "This is just terrific.
We're building our company and it's going to
be that much better because of this person." It's still
that way even after all these years.*

*I learned from working with the wrong people,
too. When I first came in, there was one guy that I
immediately didn't identify with. I was in the office
on a Saturday or Sunday and some clients came in.
This agent said to them something like "We have a
bazillion houses for sale but there is only one house
left in Seattle that fits your needs, and I'm going to
take you there." He had a habit — he would
always cough when he was exaggerating or lying.
I listened to him feeding these people such baloney
and coughing, coughing, coughing. I'd seen the
house he was trying to sell them, and it was a dog.
It was the wrong house for these people. The guy
was a liar, and we got rid of him right away.*

John Jacobi

PROVIDE A GREAT ENVIRONMENT

One of John Jacobi's first actions was to
radically change the look and atmosphere of
his offices. The shabby space he bought in
1972 was typical of the real estate business,
and this made zero sense to him. He believed
that people who worked at Windermere
deserved the best and should feel proud to
walk in the door. Clients, and anyone else who
visited, should be impressed by the efforts
made to help them feel at ease.

He insisted that the physical surroundings
be gracious and welcoming. To that end, he
made the space light and bright. Furniture
and accessories were chosen for comfort and to
please the eye. Sterility was to be avoided, and
so art became fundamental to the décor. These
changes contributed significantly to the public
perception of Windermere and, in no small
way, to agents' attitudes and understanding of
their commanding position in the business.

*The Lake Forest
Park office,
near Seattle*

Jeanne Grainger, Maria Bunting, Jim Shapiro,
Bill Feldman, Steven Kieburtz,
and John Jacobi gather for a meeting in the
early days of the Services Company.

Setting Our Own Course

3

How Can We Do a Better Job for Our People?

Perhaps the most exceptional and effective aspect of Windermere's development was the decision to stay out of the agents' way and allow them to do their best work. The corollary, then, was the need to clear their path of obstacles. John Jacobi didn't want his real estate offices mired in the search for telephone systems or wrangling with government regulations or wasting their time meeting with health insurance salespeople.

Don Deasy, who had joined Jacobi at the start, came up with the concept for a services company. The idea was to provide Windermere offices with the essentials for efficient operation and to give agents resources and materials that would make their jobs easier and more satisfying.

Don Deasy and John Jacobi had been fraternity brothers at the University of Washington with Jim Shapiro. One day in

1983, Deasy and Shapiro met for lunch and fleshed out how a services company might operate. Shapiro had worked for large corporations and had just left a position as an administrator at what he describes as a "high-flying company with huge amounts of money and equally huge administrative needs." When that company was sold to an even bigger one, he was ready for a change.

Over lunch, Deasy and Shapiro agreed that the skills required matched Jim's experience — and Shapiro was intrigued. He then met with Jacobi, who asked him to come aboard to create and oversee a support system for the growing company.

Shapiro recalls, "I came to work and sat at an agent's desk. John came in with a piece of blue paper from state government. He said, 'I don't know what this is. Why don't you try to figure it out?' That was my introduction. John knew that in order for the company to grow, the administration side would need glue. He needed somebody who didn't have the day-to-day job of running the real estate company. When I first started, I bought all the signs, I bought supplies, I bought phone systems, and

I did it for all the offices. We got good value because we could bundle it all together. John's view was that it was the agent who piloted the ship, so lots of effort and energy went toward 'How can we do a better job for our people?' Because they're the ones who are going to make the company successful."

Windermere Services grew not only because the company grew but also because Shapiro discovered more and better ways to help agents. Areas of support were added and became distinct entities that were continually refined and improved. The Services Company hired people with specific expertise in advertising and marketing, education, and technology. Individuals with extensive real estate experience joined Services to offer their wisdom to offices and agents. And in the early 1990s, it was the Services Company that pioneered what was then a techno-toy into what has become the polished, user-friendly Windermere Web site — a powerhouse tool for agents and clients.

John Jacobi and Jim Shapiro were in charge of expansion and the acquisition of franchises. At that time, they were deeply involved in developing the company and were not in any big hurry to seek out new associates. Steven Kieburtz, one of the earliest partners, describes the attitude at that time: "The only thing we ever heard, that we ever talked about, was 'Let's make this the best real estate company it can possibly be. Let's see if we can elevate the level of practice.' We never put any pins in a map and said, 'We have to expand into Ephrata next month.' "

Bill Feldman was hired to expand Windermere into new territory.

By 1988, when it became obvious that the company needed to grow, Jacobi and Shapiro

looked for an individual who could represent the Windermere way of doing business to potential prospects. They chose Bill Feldman, who had co-owned a real estate company in Spokane.

"We called him Captain Service," Shapiro says. "Bill bleeds Windermere blue. He has a really good sense of people, a very good sense of the heart of people. He was never someone just out to carve notches into his belt. Not only was he a great representative, but he was always so in tune with the client. He established true *relationships* with them. He's still active in the business, but like me, he's in the role of elder statesman. He's an adviser to both old and new affiliates. And what's so valuable is that when issues arise and problems need working out, Bill does that very well. He has a history with so many folks."

Bill Feldman, commonly known as Captain Service, is dressed in character for one of many Windermere networking events.

In Bill Feldman's own words: "We didn't have a plan to become dominant in the Northwest, but we did it because we built a network of great people. Each time we added a new Windermere office, that office opened a door with someone else. Then that person would recommend somebody good, and that's how it happened. There's never been a time when I had a quota to fill. In 1988, we had 36 offices. Now, we have more than 300 in the western U.S. and Canada. That's pretty remarkable. The reason this has happened is that we've been truly fortunate to find people who believe in what Windermere Real Estate is all about — who believe as we do that this is a relationship business, a personal business. We're not just selling houses; we're doing our best to make this a company of which everyone can be proud. Our clients feel that way. Our agents feel that way. Our owners feel that way. It's the biggest possible win-win."

Shapiro succinctly describes the mission of Windermere Services this way: "Our responsibility is for *all* of Windermere Real Estate, so the common good is most important to us. We take care of relationships, and that's why we're successful."

DOMINATE. DIFFERENTIATE.

At the beginning of Jacobi's ownership, when there were only seven or eight salespeople, he faced the immediate challenge of gaining recognition and awareness. How could his small company compete with the much bigger, established companies that had a lot of marketing money to spend? His solution was to go out and buy 10 Open House signs for each of his agents. For a negligible expenditure,

"Windermere" appeared everywhere in a potential client's neighborhood of choice; the area was quite simply blanketed with the name.

Vince Haugerud recalls this first shrewd move, as the company began to shake things up by addressing the stodgy, inconsistent marketing and advertising of real estate: "Before John came in, we were still using old red-and-white signs; some of them were supplied by a dairy company and their name was on them. One of the first things John did was to create signage for his  company that was individualistic. It was the image of the company. Create a strong, professional impression and back it up. You put those blue-and-white signs out in the neighborhood and then what you see is Windermere, Windermere, Windermere. That gets the public's attention, and when they want to do real estate business, our name is what they remember."

Don Deasy puts it this way: "You may be small potatoes in the bigger picture, but if you have a position of 70 open-house signs out in a neighborhood on a Sunday, you dominate."

And that was just the start of Jacobi's marketing and advertising philosophy: Dominate. Differentiate. Jacobi learned this from his father, who was with the Seattle advertising agency Cole & Weber. Lee Jacobi advised, "Dominate even when you aren't dominant." Applying this first tenet, John Jacobi created omnipresent open-house signage, followed by other creative ways to "own" a medium in advertising. The senior Jacobi offered another simple yet powerful suggestion: "Don't do it because others are doing it. Set your own course."

Acting on his father's advice, John Jacobi radically changed Windermere's creative approach in its newspaper advertising. Newspapers' real-estate sections were the primary medium for the business, and companies filled these pages with small "scatter" ads. There were so many, in such a multitude of styles — lots of them ridiculous and some downright ugly — that Jacobi knew they weren't effective. He wouldn't advertise his company that way. His solution was to buy the largest display ads he could afford, and consequently, Windermere broke through the clutter, both dominating and differentiating.

The history of Windermere's advertising design is not all glorious — some ads were definitely clunkers. But the company learned from its mistakes, and Windermere soon had its own distinct style. The layouts were clean, elegant, and easy to read and offered complete information about the properties.

"It helped us a lot, designing our ads specifically for people reading the Sunday paper, whether they're looking for a house or their house is for sale or maybe they just want to see what's going on in their neighborhood," Jacobi says. "There's great institutional value to that. The way the ad looks and reads — our style of advertising — is a very large part of our culture and our marketing program.

"When we started this, a lot of competitors' ads didn't list price. Now, why on earth would you want to aggravate buyers by not giving them what they most want and need — price and location? Buyers don't need to be tricked into calling a real estate office. If the price and location seem right, they'll call you!

A lot of our competitors did 'You gotta see this one! Hurry, hurry! It won't last! It's a beauty!' And that's their whole ad. In my opinion, the public's reaction to that is 'slick real estate trying to make the dough.' We delivered real information. We had the number of bedrooms, baths, square footage, trying to be as descriptive as possible."

For the first time, not only were price and location given, but Windermere also sorted available properties geographically and placed them together in an appealing, easy-to-comprehend ad rather than scattering them throughout the paper. For Jacobi, this was simply logical.

Windermere also made targeted buys on television, cable, and radio to establish or further solidify its reputation in a community. It was not the first real-estate company to use broadcast, but it was the first to eliminate self-aggrandizing claims from its advertising. Jacobi explains, "We have a competitor who can't get himself on television or anywhere else without practically breaking his right arm patting himself on the back, saying how great they are. We tried some of that, but I just didn't feel good about it. That is not our culture. Actions really do speak louder than words, and you shouldn't be in a position of having to *tell* the public how great you are. When your clients and people who've received your services say it spontaneously, without a script, it doesn't get any better."

Beginning in the early 1990s, Windermere commercials on television, cable, and radio were striking in their honesty. People volunteered their own stories, and those stories spoke volumes about the company's service and values. It was financially impossible to dominate a broadcast medium. However, by producing compelling messages, Windermere could leave a lasting impression that candidly reflected the culture of the company.

The savvy marketing pioneered and nurtured in Seattle can be taken as a powerful model. Windermere has achieved a market share of well over 40 percent in the greater Seattle area. Historically, this is more than three times that of competitors.

Advertising
Through the Years

Seattle Times *classified ad from 1987*

Magazines from the early 1990s

Institutional ad from the late 1990s

Institutional ad, 2007

2004 Premier
Living *magazine*

Personal Marketing Newsletters and Postcards Through the Years

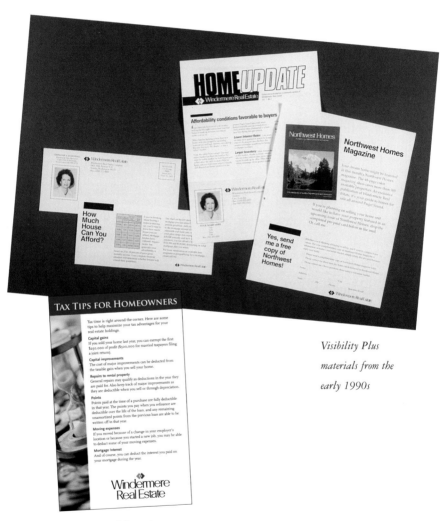

Visibility Plus materials from the early 1990s

Visibility Plus postcard from the early 2000s

2007 Home Update

newsletter

Home Update

650 · Volume 27 · Issue 01

Current real estate and market trends from Windermere

Take Advantage of a Changing Market

Over the past five years, the United States real estate market has experienced record sales and price appreciation. The real estate boom has been especially strong in the West, with home values doubling and even tripling in some cities.

Real estate is cyclical. In some areas, particularly those that have seen annual appreciation rates of 20 percent and more a year, the real estate market is cycling back to more normal conditions.

The normalizing of home prices is a natural part of the real estate cycle. It's also healthy for the market, serving to rebalance supply and demand, and bring prices more in line with what consumers can afford.

Remember that housing markets are all local. At the height of the real estate boom, some areas of the country experienced annual appreciation rates in just the low single digits. And even in regions that are seeing home prices moderate today, there are properties in highly-desirable neighborhoods that continue to receive multiple offers.

What's important is how to make the best possible real estate deal in your market.

continued on page 2

Real estate is local. Since the real estate climate varies by neighborhood, what is important is what's happening in your market. Conditions can also change quickly, so you need the most up-to-date information available to make a well-informed decision. If you're thinking of buying or selling a home, contact me for an overview of current market conditions. I can determine the value of your existing home or help you estimate the cost of a home in a neighborhood you may be considering.

Jane Agent & Joe Agent
Real Estate Professionals
REALTORS®
Jane: 206/527-3801
JaneAgent@windermere.com
Joe: 206/527-3801
JoeAgent@windermere.com
www.JaneandJoe.myWindermere.com

Windermere Real Estate

INTERNAL COMMUNICATIONS
THROUGH THE YEARS

1987 Weekly
newsletter

1993 Weekly
newsletter

1997 News & Views

magazine

2006 Blueprint

online newsletter

Diving into Technology

Jeanne Grainger came to work for Windermere Services in 1988 as director of communications. She shared the first computer, a tiny Mac, with the secretary. This one Macintosh began a revolution. For Grainger, the Mac and its increasingly sophisticated successors gave her tools that saved time and made her work easier.

Jeanne Grainger

The advent of new technology also caused Brian Allen (who then worked for Services and is now an owner of 12 offices in Oregon) to become intrigued by cyberspace and its possibilities. As he read and researched, he became an enthusiastic proponent of the Internet's incredible value to the future of both the real estate industry and Windermere. He presented the idea to John Jacobi, who neither liked nor trusted computers but saw the potential. Allen began his pursuit.

When Services started its exploration of cyberspace, there were only a few sites on the Internet, and the public was just beginning to go online. The Windermere Web site quickly became a destination as people discovered how helpful it could be. The company was also the first to provide a searchable database of properties for sale, which proved to be a hugely valuable tool for consumers. The news media took notice, and Windermere received a great deal of press coverage for daring to use this newfangled information source.

Brian Allen

As wonderful as the result has been, the start-up was anything but easy. The learning curve was steep and included terms that were like a foreign language. The new users at Windermere were often confused and frustrated because the system didn't always work correctly or because they couldn't figure it out. Agents and employees would finally arrive at a point of comfort just as a new technology was introduced, and the process would start all over again.

*Windermere graces
the cover of the
November 1996 issue
of* Washington
CEO *magazine.*

This harrowing phase was also exciting. Windermere Services' phones rang constantly because it seemed that everyone wanted to know about this innovation. In 1997, the Windermere Web site got about 5,000 hits a month. Over the years, this has grown well into the millions, and continues to increase. Brian Allen says, "It was, in a way, serendipity. It was a convergence of need, desire, technology, and the guts to take a risk."

*The original
home page of
Windermere.com*

DARING

Don't go there just because somebody else has gone there. Set the bar higher.

Don Deasy

Changing the game, risking something
new, thinking creatively, attacking
problems — without this spirit of daring,
Windermere would likely have struggled
along for a while and maybe even have gone
under during the Seattle real estate depression
of the early 1980s. Instead, Windermere
thrived, expanded, and raised the bar for
the industry.

Don Deasy sets the bar with his fashionable golf attire at a tournament in the early 1980s.

Innovation has always been a Windermere
hallmark: services companies to support
agents, Jacobi's way of partnering and fran-
chising, comfortable and inviting office spaces,
treating agents as valued professionals. The list
is long. These innovations certainly created
a better place to work. Many of them changed
the real estate business itself. What started as
Windermere ingenuity was copied by others,
and eventually became industry standards.

It is a part of John Jacobi's nature — and the company's nature — to value good people. Jacobi, his early partners, and now the new generation of Windermere owners aggressively recruit the best talent. The next step in having the best is to then take exceptional care of them. Windermere was a pioneer in providing health-care and retirement benefits for agents long before competitors even considered it.

"We make sure our people understand how important they are," John Jacobi explains. "Without them, we have nothing. We have zero."

During the 1980s, Jacobi shook up real estate by offering a better commission structure for agents. Because he believed that entrepreneurial motivation made for happier, more productive agents, he discarded the traditional 50/50-split rule. Rejecting the rigid imperative that the broker took half the commission and the agent the other half, he instead offered a graduated scale. At Windermere, the 50/50 split remained in effect only until an agent reached a specified goal. Once that goal was met, the split became 80/20 in favor of the agent. This structure not only substantially rewarded the top producers, but it also attracted the best and most successful agents into the Windermere fold. A few years later, the company sweetened the deal even more in some of its offices, making it possible for an agent to keep 100 percent.

A June 1987 Seattle Times *article*

"We wanted to give agents the opportunity to make as much money as possible," Jacobi says. "We always said we wanted to pay them better, and we went ahead and proved it. True entrepreneurship is the fire in Windermere."

Windermere also devised groundbreaking ways to help its clients. The concept of the "guaranteed sale" was yet another innovation that confounded the industry. Though revolutionary, the idea was simple. It developed during the booming market of the late 1970s, when contingent offers could undo clients' proposals for a home they wanted. Windermere decided to "guarantee" the sale of a buyer's present home. That is, the company promised to purchase the house at a given date for a given price if the property hadn't sold. Erasing the contingency was a great boon to clients, giving them peace of mind in placing an unburdened offer.

What seemed a big risk to observers simply was not. It was savvy common sense. In a hot housing market, there was very little downside. Windermere did it because

Windermere could, and thereby won clients and their loyalty.

This same innovative thinking inspired a logical corollary: the bridge loan. Now an industry standard, it was brand-new thinking at the time and another great benefit for clients. Rather than guarantee the sale as it had in the flourishing market, Windermere offered an independently financed loan for buyers, engineered by the company. This meant that even without the guarantee, customers would not have to risk losing a house they wanted because their current home was still on the market.

Despite the many risks the company has taken, there is one area where John Jacobi didn't want to take any. "I hate debt," he says. "I'm a strong believer in putting a buck in the bank for a rainy day. Controlling expenses thoroughly and tightly is paramount to succeeding in business. Without tough oversight, you're just looking at struggle. Keeping costs down is what allows the new ideas and bold experiments to happen in the first place."

PERSONAL MARKETING

Personal marketing has become immensely important for agents because they are independent contractors. I think that one of the major reasons they choose Windermere over our competitors is that we have a reputation for terrific marketing materials and support.

Because agents are independent, and tastes and styles vary so much, their marketing can also vary a great deal. What some agents do in creating their own newsletters or other materials is very good, but some can be pretty bad. I think it's important to address the problems rather than overlook them just because it might be uncomfortable.

For instance, there have been agents who refer to themselves as "Mr. or Mrs. Real Estate." In my opinion, this is unprofessional, and we work very hard to get them to change their approach. You wouldn't visit a dentist who calls himself "Dr. Root Canal."

*We also don't want to leave agents out there
hanging, spending their valuable time and money
trying to come up with their own concepts. So we
have a great bunch of creative and design people to
help out. We have direct-mail programs and a lot of
other materials to support personal marketing.
Probably most important in this day and age is the
Internet. We do everything we can to make sure that
our agents can secure a meaningful presence there.
It's hugely important for us to help agents establish
their business in conjunction with our business.
We're partners.*

John Jacobi

*"Just Listed" Custom
Xpress postcard*

Windermere began the tradition of celebrating Community Service Day in 1984.

A Deeply Held Belief

4

"LET'S GET INVOLVED."

As with all things Jacobi, caring for and giving
back to the community began with an insight
that became a deeply held belief. Early on,
John got a call asking if Windermere would
sponsor a junior symphony. He said "sure" and
then kept on going, becoming intensely and
substantially involved in the community.

In the beginning, the company supported
many different organizations and activities,
from Little League teams to school projects to
a wide range of nonprofit groups. These early
efforts evolved into something much bigger
because Windermere was inspired to help
more people and increase participation. Rather
than these well-intentioned but scattered
efforts, everyone would work together on one
encompassing and meaningful event.

That's how Windermere's Community
Service Day was born in 1984. Agents, staff,
management, and owners choose a day to offer

*Vince Haugerud,
John Jacobi, and
Sharon Henry at
Community Service
Day in 1986*

special skills plus manual labor to clean,
restore, rebuild, refurbish, and otherwise help
out the many schools and groups that are in
desperate need of these services. The projects
are especially rewarding because they stay
close to home. All the work takes place in the
areas where offices are located, for people who
are Windermere's neighbors.

In his inimitable style, Jacobi describes
the first Community Service Day: "Let's get
involved. Let's show that we care. If we don't
really care, then the hell with it, we won't do
it. But we *did* care. And we weren't looking
for publicity. We didn't get any. What we did
get was a really good feeling from everybody.
It was a path we started down that's evolved
into what it is today. And I think that's
profoundly important for our culture."

Community Service Day is a Windermere
tradition that has served neighborhoods and
communities for more than 20 years. Dick
Wood, owner of the Lynnwood office, says,
"Our agents are 100 percent behind our
community involvement. It feels good to relate
to each other on a different level, and it *really*
feels good to give back to the community.
We've had agents with tears in their eyes when
we've gone to shelters for battered women and
painted the place and built new toys for the
kids and just helped out. To see the faces of
these people after you've done that for them,
when the rest of the world is kind of kicking
them in the teeth . . . it's pretty special."

*Jill Jacobi Wood at
Community Service
Day in 1994*

"It was a wonderful day. One wonderful day."
Our children are little tiny people with some kind of handicap. They'll have spina bifida, Down syndrome, cerebral palsy, all types of heartbreaking disabilities. They come to us from birth to three years old. When we get them, their parents have all the sad information about what their kids will never be able to do. We work with these babies. We give them their hope back.

Windermere has been helping us for a long time. They come out all charged up to work all day until they get everything done that's on our list. They've washed windows, weeded and cleaned up the play yard, the garden, and our pond. They even got us new fish. They painted, and a group of them even came in the office and did computer work that we needed. It was a wonderful day. One wonderful day.

I don't know if they know how thankful we are. By doing things we can't afford to pay for, they literally keep us going.

Barb George

Little Red School House

"This might be the first time in their lives they've felt that adults care about them."

I think the biggest challenge in this country is helping kids, especially kids who have been abused. They need our help. Ryther is a home for children struggling with physical and sexual abuse, drug addiction, and mental illness. We're a place of last resort. The kids here are overwhelmed when they see a group of adults come in and roll up their sleeves and just get down and do completely dirty work. A lot of kids have never seen grown-ups working for the benefit of others. This might be the first time in their lives they've felt that adults care about them.

Windermere just wants to make their community a better place.

Gary Lange
Ryther Child Center

"They get to see that people care about them."
We provide critical services and shelter for homeless teens. Most of the kids we serve have seen domestic violence or been victims of physical and sexual abuse. We bring services to them on-site — counseling, medical care, and help for any substance abuse. We also get them back to education so that all the kids are working toward their high school diplomas or are in a GED program.

Windermere volunteers came over and climbed tall ladders and painted the entire outside of our building. They cleaned up the yard, pruned bushes, mowed the lawn. These kids have been disappointed a lot and they don't have much and people have generally not done much for them. The wonderful thing about Community Service Day is that they get to see that people care about them. It sends a strong message not only of respect for the place where they live but that they're respected, too. The Windermere agents are passionate about these kids. They have a huge heart for the community.

Petrina Lin
Cocoon House

THE POWER TO CHANGE LIVES

In 1989, Windermere was enjoying strong and steady growth in Western Washington. Each office had participated in Community Service Day and witnessed the tremendous impact this one event had on communities and neighborhoods. Windermere offices also gave money to many groups and causes, as did their agents and employees. But these good-hearted efforts caused many within Windermere to ask whether they'd made *enough* of a difference.

Community Service Day was a success, but the people of Windermere wanted to do more. In response, John Jacobi established a parallel program for financial assistance that would have real power to change lives. To head up this effort he chose a smart, fiercely determined agent he knew would get the job done right.

Maria Bunting had worked in the original office since 1987, and when presented with this task, she hit the ground running. She did the research, including canvassing community leaders to assess what they perceived as the greatest areas of

Maria Bunting brought the Windermere Foundation to life.

need. She conferred with Windermere's
attorney, John Coart, who worked on the
project *pro bono*, and visited all the offices to
present the idea. Within two months, the
Windermere Foundation became a reality,
with the goal of helping homeless and low-
income families and children.

The first Foundation endeavor was so
ambitious that it eventually proved unsustain-
able. The plan was to buy houses as residences
for families who were leaving transitional
shelters. The Windermere House project
started with the purchase of three homes. It
was a wonderful idea, but had so many
complex problems that the company soon
realized it could help only a few of the many

who needed aid and shelter. Benefiting from
this honorable failure, the Foundation moved
on to work with nonprofit organizations so that
help would reach as many families as possible.

The basic model for funding the
Windermere Foundation is ingenious. Agents
donate a portion of their commission from
each transaction, guaranteeing the growth and
longevity of the fund without being a financial
burden for any individual. Over time, this
method has evolved so that a good amount of
the income is derived from fund-raisers and
over-and-above donations. In the first year, the
Windermere Foundation raised $90,000.
In 2005, it brought in more than $2 million,
while keeping administrative costs at less
than 2 percent.

Although the Foundation was never self-
aggrandizing, word got out. Agents reported
getting calls from buyers and sellers who knew
about the donations. They saw Windermere
in a different light, as unique in the business.
One agent told Bunting, "It makes clients
respect Windermere. It makes people happy to
do business with us."

To ensure that the Foundation is meaningful for Windermere agents everywhere, local offices choose organizations to support in their own areas. Over the years, the Foundation has succeeded in making a significant difference where it counts the most — in the neighborhoods that Windermere serves.

Maria Bunting explains, "Commitment to community came from John Jacobi when he started Windermere. He believes that all successful people should give back. The Windermere Foundation allows everyone in the company to do tremendous good. It's just a natural part of our culture. When you see pictures of children enjoying camp for the first time, or adults getting assistance to get the education they need . . . sometimes it's just the really simple things like new shoes for the first day of school. You watch these kids trying on the shoes and smiling, and it makes your heart sing to know you were a part of that."

I have a very bittersweet job. I hear really sad stories. I get calls from moms living in their cars and that's really difficult to take because I'm a mom, too. But I keep reminding myself that the

Windermere Foundation is part of the solution and that we're actually helping these families who are in such desperate, frightening situations.

Christine Wood
Executive Director
Windermere Foundation

Christine Wood with children from the YMCA

"Bring your babies in."
The Community Health Center provides affordable, high-quality health care for people who are uninsured or underinsured — for those who could not otherwise afford help when they need it most. I want to quote one of our moms describing her feeling of despair when she wakes up in the middle of the night with a very sick child . . . she's low income, she's uninsured. She said, "I wait, I watch, I worry, I pray. And when I can wait no longer, then I'll go to the hospital emergency room. And then, I wait and pray again because I know I'm not going to be able to pay the bill. But because CHC is here, now I have a choice." The Windermere Foundation helps to support our children's program. They help make that choice a reality.

There really are no words to describe how I feel when I hear the voices of thankful moms, when I can say, "Come on, bring that child in. It doesn't matter that you can't pay today. Bring your babies in. We'll take care of them. We'll work it out."

Windermere certainly is represented by the Foundation. But they're also wonderfully represented by their agents, who are so engaged with the community.

Peg Crowley

Community Health Center

"It's more than money."

It's hard to convey the sense of despair that families feel when they become homeless. Our Windermere-sponsored transitional housing units are a godsend — a safe place where families can rebuild their lives. Despair is replaced by a sense of hope and a conviction that the community cares about them. They begin to believe that they can accomplish their dreams.

What Windermere gives is more than money. It's about people and connectedness and caring and love.

Ed Petersen

Housing Hope

"Windermere has shown a dedication to our community that is incomparable."

So many of the kids we work with have been either physically or emotionally abused by an adult they once trusted. It's usually very bad circumstances for them at home, and they either are forced out or run away. With no place to go, they end up on the streets.

One thing we've recognized after working with these kids is that education is their escape from a dead-end existence. Once they get a high school equivalency diploma and some job training, most of them can live independently. In fact, upwards of 75 percent of the young people who attend our school graduate and get a job. Some have even gone on to college.

The Windermere Foundation has been with us from the very beginning. They helped us build a transitional-housing facility where our kids can be safe and secure. Then, they helped us expand our school.

Windermere has shown a dedication to our community that is incomparable. In many respects, we consider them our best friends.

Ken Cowdery

New Avenues for Youth

CONNECTING

Cities, towns, and neighborhoods have their own distinctive personalities. Their citizens gather and celebrate occasions that reveal exactly who they are.

As a good neighbor, Windermere forges strong local connections in the neighborhoods where it is privileged to belong. Windermere supports and sponsors the grassroots events that its communities care about.

The Windermere Cup, a rowing regatta established in Seattle in 1987, was the first such sponsorship. It's a great example of how the company — in whatever city or town — gets enthusiastically involved with events that bring people together in a meaningful way.

In the Seattle area, great bodies of water define and inform a way of life. So it was a natural for Windermere to become involved in Opening Day of boating season, a tradition that began in 1913. Every year on the first Saturday in May, tens of thousands of people line the shore of the Montlake Cut, a narrow waterway flowing by the University of Washington and connecting Lake Washington to Lake Union. They come to watch hundreds of boats — sleek million-dollar yachts with passengers dressed in conservative attire alongside wildly decorated boats piloted by pirates, clowns, and garage bands.

The Windermere Cup Races

1987 Opening Day Regatta

Opening Day Legend

IMA = Intramural
GLC = Green Lake Crew
Brentwood = Brentwood College
Shawnigan = Shawnigan School
Hillside = Hillside High School
Mt. Baker = Mt. Baker Rowing & Sailing
Everett RC = Everett Rowing Club
Redwood = Redwood Crew
Seattle YC = Seattle Yacht Club
Western JC = Western Junior Crew
Meydenbauer YC = Meydenbauer Bay Yacht Club
Corinthian YC = Corinthian Yacht Club
Tacoma YC = Tacoma Yacht Club
Conibear YC = Conibear Yacht Club
Seattle RC = Seattle Rowing Club
LWRC = Lake Washington Rowing Club
Rainier RA = Rainier Rowing Association

UW = University of Washington
PLU = Pacific Lutheran University
WSU = Washington State University
SPU = Seattle Pacific University
HRC = Husky Rowing Club
M. Mom's = Martha's Mom's
WSP = Washington State Patrol
LASO = Los Angeles Sheriff's Office
OSU = Oregon State University
UC-SD = University of California San Diego
UBC = University of British Columbia
USA = USA National Team Candidates
Canada = Canadian National Team Candidates
Edgewater = Edgewater High School (Orlando, Fl.)
California = University of California, Berkeley
WWU = Western Washington University
USSR = Soviet Union

The first Windermere Cup program, from 1987

The 1997 Husky
men's crew team

Since the 1970s, crew racing had kicked off the Opening Day celebration in the morning. This was a homegrown event featuring the UW against other West Coast college teams. That changed in 1986, when Blaine Newnham, a columnist for the *Seattle Times*, wrote an article asserting that the crew races could and should be so much more. Newnham hoped that someone from the private sector would step up and make the races a higher-profile event.

John Jacobi read the article and talked to UW Athletic Director Mike Lude and legendary coach Dick Erickson. Together, they decided not only to make the crew races a world-class event, but also to increase their worldwide importance by inviting the Soviet Union team. This was during *glasnost,* and it was the first time in many long years that any Russian sports team had visited the States.

The 2001 Windermere Cup champions are featured in the Tacoma News Tribune.

Members of the Washington women's varsity eight whoop it up after beating the Romanian national crew in 6 minutes, 17.12 seconds to win the Windermere Cup. It was the third-fastest time ever.

Dave J. Kopman/The News Tribune

Just call it ladies day

At the completion of the race, the Husky and Soviet teams quickly shuffled their oarsmen. Each shell contained a mix of Americans and Russians, and they rowed together back down the Cut, to the delight of the spectators. As a symbol of great sportsmanship, this moment still lives in the hearts of all who were there for the very first Windermere Cup.

Windermere has provided long-standing support for crew racing, a demanding sport that requires the utmost in teamwork and dedication. The company's involvement has grown to include the Bay Area's Windermere Real Estate Rowing Classic, which since 2003 has partnered Windermere with Stanford University.

Whether it is supporting a sporting event, a local festival, or the fine arts, Windermere's desire has always been — and always will be — to make meaningful and personal connections with its communities.

The Windermere Cup

For each Windermere
Cup, an original
piece of artwork
is commissioned and
featured in a
commemorative poster.

Maria Bunting, Steven Rieburtz, Don Deasy,
April Rieburtz, Jim Shapiro,
John Jacobi, Dick Baldwin, and Bill Feldman
attend the dedication ceremony
for the Terry Haberbush memorial rowing shell.

5

The Windermere Way

Stay Calm. Smile.

Most Important, Have Fun.

If companies have personalities — and most assuredly, they do — then Windermere is a nimble, brainy contender with a good heart, a stubborn allegiance to integrity, and a belief in the power of trusting human relationships.

This book illustrates that "The Windermere Way" is in fact the core beliefs held by those who pioneered the company. These values still run deep among the current owners and agents. The culture is personal and relevant each day. For that reason, it's certain to endure.

Throughout his years with Windermere, John Jacobi has sought the wisdom of smart and inspiring people — parents, authors, tycoons, teachers, and business-management gurus. Some of this advice has particularly resonated with him, and has struck a chord within Windermere as well.

In Their Own Words

Matt Crile: "Crawl. Walk. Run."

I came to work for Windermere Services in 1997. After three years, I talked to John Jacobi and Jim Shapiro and told them that I would love to be an owner, although I didn't see how that would be possible. But they seemed to take this dream of mine and make it their own. In 2001, the owner of the Hillsboro, Oregon, office decided to sell his brokerage. They thought I'd be good there. I was exhilarated to the point of terror, but I jumped at the opportunity. I trusted the wisdom of those around me.

Matt Crile

When I took over in Hillsboro, I was reminded
constantly of John's counsel: "Crawl, walk, run."
Each change, every improvement, all forward motion
required the patient application of this advice.
Improving your financials? Crawl, walk, run.
Growing your office? Providing new services?
Building your market share? Crawl, walk, run.
Our fundamental objective — to develop partner-
ships with career-minded agents who see themselves
as business owners first and foremost — is never
compromised in a crawl, walk, run environment.

When I think about the Windermere Way, it is
not systems or theory or structure that comes to mind.
It is the names, faces, and personalities of people
who stand behind the brand. For me, it was and
continues to be the interactions with the founders,
the pioneering executives, the earliest owners, the
second-generation leaders, and — above all — the
Windermere agents that define the organization and
inform my decisions on its behalf.

It is my highest professional hope that I might
one day help to characterize this organization for
tomorrow's leaders.

This book would not be complete without including some of the "Jacobi-isms" that have become so familiar to his friends and coworkers. John Jacobi is quick to point out that very few of these words of wisdom are original. But they have become some of Windermere's favorite commonsense guidelines — or more familiarly, "J.J.'s Way."

Like father, like son (see page 5). John Jacobi and wife Roz show their "Aloha Spirit" at one of many festive family costume parties.

J.J.'s Way

Either do it right or don't do it.

Take risks. Don't play it safe.

Don't be afraid to make mistakes.
   Don't try to avoid them.

Take initiative. Don't wait for instructions.

Spend energy on solutions, not emotions.
   Don't waste time obsessing about the problem.

Shoot for total quality. Don't shave standards.

Break things. Welcome destruction.
   It's the first step to the creative process.

Experiment. Not everything works the first time.

Take personal responsibility for fixing things.
   Don't blame others.

Keep it simple. Make it easier rather than harder.

Stay calm. Smile. And most important — have fun.

Acknowledgments

My family, especially my wife, Roz, have
all been a profound part of this Windermere
story. My kids have done everything from
sweeping the sidewalks to running the show.
I am very grateful to them that we have
not only familial relationships but also
trusting friendships.

Roz Jacobi
Jill and Geoff Wood
Cathy Sherris
John "O.B." Jacobi
Tori and Carter Dotson
Meredith and Doug Betzold
Molly and Mike Pitts

The Jacobi family in 1981: Tori, Meredith, Jill, Molly, Cathy, O.B. (and Sheba)

The Jacobi family in 2006 on a fishing trip in Big Bay, British Columbia